Original title:
Oaks and Oddities

Copyright © 2025 Creative Arts Management OÜ
All rights reserved.

Author: Sophia Kingsley
ISBN HARDBACK: 978-1-80567-411-5
ISBN PAPERBACK: 978-1-80567-710-9

## Dreamscapes Beneath Acanthous Leaves

Underneath the leafy crown,
Danced a squirrel in a gown.
Chasing shadows, lost in glee,
Whispering secrets to a bee.

Raucous laughter fills the air,
As mushrooms don their finest fare.
A hedgehog winks with a wise old grin,
While whispering tales of where he's been.

## Fables Adrift in Ruined Boughs

In a nook where branches twist,
A forgotten frog made a list.
Not of stones or flies to catch,
But of dreams that never match.

A parrot with a pirate's fear,
Crooned jokes for all who'd hear.
It squawked in rhymes and silly tunes,
While time dripped like melting moons.

## The Artistry of Distortion and Design

A painter critiqued a crooked twig,
Said it looked like a dancing pig.
The pine trees chuckled and swayed along,
As the wind joined in with a whimsical song.

Rusty gears from a clock ran wild,
Pondering life as a lost, grown child.
They ticked and tocked in the funniest way,
Helping old stories still have their play.

## Enigma Amongst the Greenery

A wise old turtle spun a tale,
Of a cat who thought it could sail.
With a hat made of leaves and a grin so wide,
It paddled a puddle on a sunny slide.

The flowers giggled, dressed in flair,
Claiming to act like they just don't care.
A rabbit juggled acorns with grace,
While beetles snapped selfies at a wild pace.

## Explorations in the Abstract Wood

In the forest where the shadows dance,
Trees wear hats, they take a chance.
Squirrels gossip in silly tones,
While mushrooms chat on their tiny phones.

A snail tries on a pair of shoes,
Says he'll cruise, but he'll refuse.
The sun laughs, a cheeky grin,
As butterflies twirl in a silly spin.

## The Bizarre Beauty of the Grove

A walrus painted in bright pink,
Sips on juice, demands a drink.
Dancing frogs in bright green capes,
Hold the party for strange landscapes.

Curly vines throw confetti chews,
As raccoons skip in polka shoes.
The wind carries the joker's jest,
In this grove, we find the best.

## The Odd Companions of Branches

A parrot told a joke so fine,
The chickadees laughed in a straight line.
Beneath the branches of the tall trees,
Lies a snail painting with bright leaves.

A fox wearing glasses, quite debonair,
Debates with a hedgehog, spiky hair.
Together they craft the silliest tales,
As the wind tells secrets through curled up trails.

## Footprints of the Quirk

Footprints of shapes that zigzag around,
Show the route where odd things are found.
A raccoon in a tutu prances bright,
While fireflies join in, a buzzing fright.

In the underbrush, a laugh rolls out,
Who knew the mushrooms could shout?
With every step, there's something new,
In the quirk of this wood, how we grew.

## Beneath the Olden Boughs

Under branches, shadows dance,
Inhaling laughter, giving chance.
Squirrels play their acorn games,
While birds are singing silly names.

Mysteries hide in each thick trunk,
With secrets sprinkled, quite debunked.
A raccoon wears a mismatched sock,
And giggles echo like a clock.

## Strange Fruits of Imagination

Peaches wear polka-dot bow ties,
While apples boast unexpected lies.
Lemons giggle, dressed like clowns,
In a garden filled with quirky browns.

Grapes are juggling, all in sync,
With cherries sipping on cold drinks.
A mango tells a knock-knock joke,
Causing laughter to provoke.

**Tales in the Tangled Underbrush**

Old bushes twist in playful ways,
Where critters set up wild displays.
A fox, with flair, dons a cape,
And claims he's looking for escape.

Beneath the leaves, odd echoes play,
As badgers plot their grand cabaret.
A hedgehog spins like a top,
While bunnies dance, they never stop.

## The Curious Clouds Above

Above, the clouds parade around,
Dressed in hats, quite profound.
One floats low, wears a silly grin,
As if it knows where fun begins.

A puffball tickles all that it sees,
While rain drops ponder, "What's the tease?"
In this sky of giggles and cheer,
Who knew a cloud could be so dear?

## The Mosaic of the Woodland

In the forest, a squirrel wore a tie,
Chatting with a mushroom, oh my, oh my!
Bunny bakes cupcakes with a frosted swirl,
While beavers dance jigs, giving a twirl.

The fox plays chess with a wise old owl,
While raccoons plot mischief with a growl.
The trees laugh soft, with leaves all aglow,
As the woods come alive, putting on a show.

## Surreal Echoes in the Twilight


A hedgehog in glasses reads the news,
While a llama in boots taps a tune with its hooves.
The fireflies flash, like stars on a spree,
Illuminating secrets that only they see.

A cat rides a snail in a race through the grass,
While whispers of fairies, in circles they pass.
Every night brings a new dose of joy,
Where odd is the norm for each girl and boy.

## Arcane Chronicles of the Forest

In a hollow old tree, a wizard did dwell,
Crafting odd potions with a laugh and a yell.
His assistant, a gnome with a curious grin,
Counts tiny fish swimming in a tin.

The owls debate ancient mysteries both,
While a dancing raccoon sings an oath.
Magic abounds in the quirkiest ways,
Turning mundane moments into bright, silly days.

## Tales from the Knotted Roots

Knots in the roots, secrets unfold,
Where a wise old tortoise spins tales of bold.
The trees lend an ear to a playful hare,
Who dreams of a world with candy to share.

A parade of odd creatures strut down the lane,
With bubblegum hats and a funny refrain.
As night paints the sky with a twinkle and shine,
In this quirky realm, all is perfectly fine.

## The Lore of Lopsided Limbs

A tree with branches, askew and wide,
Bears secrets hidden, like fruit in stride.
Twisted tales dance in the summer air,
While squirrels gossip without a care.

Lopsided limbs, a quirky sight,
With acorns falling, they bring delight.
A leafy crown, it tilts with pride,
In nature's circus, the bark's the guide.

## Where Time Stands Still

In a grove where whispers seem to freeze,
Every heartbeat flutters like the leaves.
A clock with hands stuck, it winks at me,
While squirrels race in their own jubilee.

Moss carpets ground, a soft, green bed,
Where rabbits yarn tales, their ears widespread.
This funny space defies the tick,
As shadows grow and clocks play tricks.

## Phantoms of the Woodland Realm

Beneath the arches where bright shadows leap,
Giggles of phantoms that never sleep.
With twiggy fingers, they tap the ground,
In prances and laughter, their joy is found.

Whirlwinds of leaves bear stories of old,
Mischievous spirits, both cheeky and bold.
They paint the night in shades of jest,
Chasing moonbeams as they play, they're blessed.

## The Fables Woven in Leaves

Leaves rustle softly, each a tale to spin,
Of woodland wonder, where laughs begin.
Each rustle's a secret, each flutter a rhyme,
In this leafy land, there's no end to time.

With colors so bright, the stories unfold,
Of creatures so silly, they're daring and bold.
From squirrels in suits to owls that sing,
In this forest of fables, let joy take wing.

## Nature's Riddles Unfurled

In the forest where squirrels dance,
A chipmunk wears his best pants.
Trees whisper secrets, oh so sly,
While birds in ties just flutter by.

A rabbit's hat, a badger's shoe,
In a world where odd is the norm, it's true.
An owl who juggles with perfect grace,
And frogs that wear a frown on their face.

The ants hold meetings, quite profound,
Discussing how to best move around.
With winks and giggles, they plot their schemes,
In this realm of peculiar dreams.

Pinecone hats and acorn crowns,
Such silly sights bring laughter 'round.
Nature's riddles, all unfurled,
In this zany, whimsical world.

## Whimsy Amongst the Thickets

Through tangled branches, giggles peep,
Where hedgehogs tumble without a leap.
A porcupine rows a tiny boat,
While frogs compose a silly note.

A raccoon laughs at his own reflection,
As crickets plan their next perfection.
In thickets thick with joyful sights,
Where shadows dance and laughter ignites.

The earthworms boast of grounding ties,
In their underworld, odd truths arise.
With wormy wigs and smiling faces,
They celebrate in all the right places.

A hedgehog's tea party, come and see,
With cupcakes made of bark and brie.
Whimsy thrives in every nook,
In this wild, enchanted book.

## The Leafy Conundrum

Underneath the boughs so wide,
A turtle takes a funnier ride.
With a snail as partner, slow and wise,
They ponder why the days can fly.

Leaves chatter secrets of the breeze,
Spreading laughter like buzzing bees.
A mushroom wears a polka-dot hat,
While fireflies tango, oh what a spat!

In the shade where oddballs blend,
Squirrels bring their acorn trend.
Each nut a treasure, each laugh a clue,
In this leafy world, we find something new.

Peeking through the vibrant green,
A raccoon juggles what's never seen.
In the puzzle of nature, odd toys align,
Creating a riddle in every line.

**Fantastic Foliage Tales**

In the glade where shadows play,
A fox drops jokes in disarray.
Hedgehogs giggle at a silly pun,
As mushrooms cheer, "Oh, that was fun!"

A deer with glasses reads a map,
While nearby frogs perform a tap.
With stories spun in colors bright,
Each leaf a character in pure delight.

Chasing echoes through the thicket,
Bunnies find an old ballet ticket.
They leap and whirl in purest glee,
Telling tales of what may be.

Fantastic sights, oh hear the calls,
As critters gather through the halls.
With laughter shared under the sun,
Each day a new story has begun.

## **Enchanted Understory**

In shadows deep where critters play,
A dancing squirrel leads the way.
With acorns tossed, a forest feast,
The laughter rings from beast to beast.

Upon a branch, a parrot pranks,
In colored feathers, it gives its thanks.
A tiny owl with oversized eyes,
Pretends to be the sage, so wise.

The rabbits dress in leafy hats,
While hedgehogs dance with sprightly chats.
In this lush realm of whimsy bright,
The little things bring pure delight.

So if you wander, heed the cheer,
It's not just trees that grow, my dear.
Adventure calls from every nook,
So take a glance, come take a look!

## Ephemeral Roots

Beneath the ground, the mischief brews,
With whispers shared by earthworm crews.
They plot to play a little trick,
On all the passers who walk quick.

A bygone grapevine tells a tale,
Of wild confetti, winds that sail.
An acorn dreams of flying far,
While proving it's a little star.

The roots, they giggle, twist and tease,
As mushrooms wiggle in the breeze.
With every stomp upon the floor,
They wiggle back – let's have some more!

And in this place where oddities dwell,
Nature crafts tales that cast a spell.
Join in the fun, let's have a root,
As laughter echoes, take a toot!

## The Saga of Sturdy Giants

Sturdy giants, tall and grand,
Got lost in dreams of far-off land.
With their thick trunks and branches wide,
They might just hide a strange inside.

One claimed to hold a secret key,
To treasure hidden by a bee.
And while they shared a hearty laugh,
A tiny bird stole half their staff.

With knots and twists that time bestows,
These playful forms strike silly poses.
A dance-off starts with roots entwined,
Though squirrels judge, they're quite unkind.

So hear their tales, both bold and bright,
As shadows stretch in fading light.
These sturdy folks, with tales so sly,
Make every moment fly on by!

## Fables Carved in Bark

Upon the bark, the stories weave,
Of mischief meant to make us grieve.
A chipmunk dressed in dapper threads,
With acorn hats and fancy spreads.

A cunning fox, with jokes to tell,
Came by to claim the woodland's shell.
As laughter rolled, the leaves would sway,
With funny tales to end the day.

Engraved in wood, a chipper grin,
Adventures shared by kith and kin.
With every groove, a memory made,
In hallowed woods where light will fade.

So wander close, and take a peek,
At whispered tales, both witty and cheek.
For in this realm of rich delight,
The carved fables bring cheer each night!

## Oddball Musings in the Forest

In the shade where the squirrels dance,
A raccoon wears a hat by chance.
Trees whisper secrets, oh so grand,
As mushrooms giggle at the land.

A fox in socks prances about,
While owls hoot in a joyful shout.
The branches sway like hands on cue,
And bees wear shoes of vibrant hue.

With acorns bouncing on the ground,
A rabbit's juggling, quite profound.
The playful winds set leaves to twirl,
In this odd world, we laugh and whirl.

## Song of the Wildly Woven

Amidst the twigs, a tune so bright,
A frog croaks out a pure delight.
The fabric of the forest sings,
As crickets play on rubber strings.

A lizard skates on sunny rocks,
While chattering chipmunks hop in flocks.
This tapestry of silly sounds,
Unravels joy in leaps and bounds.

A snail slides by, a painter bold,
With rainbow trails, a story told.
The funky trees do twist and sway,
In nature's dance, we laugh and play.

## The Enigma of Twisted Tangles

In tangled vines, a secret lies,
A hedgehog dreams of flying high.
Lopsided oak with a crooked grin,
Hosts tiny insect parties within.

A squirrel dons a waistcoat neat,
While grasshoppers dance on dainty feet.
The sun peeks through in curious rays,
As laughter echoes through the maze.

A dandelion makes a wish,
While ants prepare a banquet dish.
With whispers soft as leaves that rustle,
Unusual moments make us chuckle.

## Reflections of the Unusual Sunlight

When sunlight sprinkles golden dew,
The flowers gossip, that much is true.
A dancing shadow makes us grin,
As butterflies waltz on a whim.

The moon joins in, a silver sprite,
In midnight talks with stars so bright.
With laughter woven through the air,
We bask in strange, delightful flair.

A porcupine spins tales of cheer,
While furry creatures gather near.
In every ray and glimmer found,
The world's odd stitches come around.

## The Mythical Options of the Canopy

Under the sky, a squirrel wears a tie,
He claims to be an investor, oh my!
With acorns in hand and dreams so grand,
He branches out to sell, isn't that a plan?

The birds debate which fruit's divine,
A peach or a nut? They sip on brine.
In shadows they plot with feathers so bright,
To open a café, quite the delightful sight!

A raccoon visits, in a suit and hat,
Says he's the chef, imagine that!
With recipes handwritten in the dirt,
His secret sauce? A dash of dessert!

Beneath the leaves, a dance did commence,
With worms as the band, it was full of suspense.
The breeze gave a laugh, the branches did sway,
Who knew tree life could be so risqué?

**Through the Lens of the Strangely Shaped**


A branch bent low, like a curious friend,
Asking me questions that never quite end.
"What's your favorite shape?" it whispery swayed,
While squirrels in bell-bottoms nervously played.

Around the trunk, a spiral so odd,
A snail in a top hat paid homage to God.
"Life's about fashion," he said with a grin,
"I'll slide through the grass, you'll never see me win!"

The shadows cast creatures, like ghosts from a dream,
With legs made of licorice—what a sweet scheme!
Then giggles erupted from pockets of air,
For fun is the treasure that's hidden somewhere.

In knotted old bark, a face seems to smirk,
Whispering gossip of each random quirk.
The humor resides in each twist and turn,
So let's raise our glasses to the wood and learn!

# The Poetry of the Unusual Twig

A twig stood tall with a strut most absurd,
Claiming to be the best poet ever heard.
It yelled 'I'll recite an ode to the wind!'
While pigeons chuckled, "Oh where to begin?"

With leaves as his pages, he scratched with delight,
Spinning tales of dreams and flights in the night.
But squirrels, with acorns, threw rhymes of their own,
A competition ensued, each verse overthrown.

"Let's have a duel!" cried the plum-hued crow,
"Bring out your best, put on a good show!"
But the twig responded, with a flourish so keen,
"Why argue with fowl? Let's dance in between!"

So under the stars in the cool evening glow,
They crafted a ball, where the oddities flow.
With laughter and music, they serenaded the trees,
A party of odd, where everyone's pleased!

## Castles Among the Twisted Barks

In fairy-tale land, where the branches are bold,
The trunks twist and curl, like stories untold.
A castle of knots, with windows of moss,
Where dreams are built high, and nothing's a loss!

The fairies play chess, on a board made of leaf,
While gnomes speak in riddles, much to my disbelief.
They argue on magic and which way to dance,
Each turn of the trunk adds a whimsical chance.

A dragon arrives, on a skateboard, quite slick,
He suggests "Let's race, but be ready for tricks!"
So off to the winds, they took flight with glee,
All for the crown of the wild canopy.

With laughter and joy, they create their own fate,
In castles of bark, where oddities wait.
Each creak and each rustle is laughter in disguise,
Among the green giants, where fun never dies.

## The Wondrous Riddles of the Understory

In a patch where shadows play,
A squirrel wears a hat today.
He shimmies up and down the bough,
Declares himself the king, and how!

A toad with glasses reads the news,
While fireflies debate their shoes.
A dancing leaf, it twirls and spins,
And laughs at how the fun begins.

The beetles argue in a row,
Which way the evening breezes blow.
They toss their tiny heads in glee,
Claiming, "Come join our jubilee!"

A raccoon snickers at the show,
Wonders if he should join or go.
With a wink to the tallest tree,
He shouts, "Come on, let's all be free!"

## **Enigmatic Leaves in Moonlight**

Under silver beams they sway,
Dancing in a nightly play.
Whispers drift on gentle breeze,
Tickling branches, teasing leaves.

Mysterious shadows loom,
Beneath the trees, a secret room.
Lively sprites with laughter bright,
Hide and seek in soft moonlight.

Frogs adorned in hats and suits,
Discuss the gossip of their roots.
The night wears wonders, strange but true,
While critters giggle, just like you.

As dusk gives way to dreams untold,
The secrets of the woods unfold.
In jumbled whispers echo clear,
The joy of oddities draws near.

## The Curious Tale of the Twisted Trunk

Once stood a trunk, all crooked and bent,
Claiming each twist as a new event.
Neighbors whispered, 'Look at that one!'
While squirrels laughed from branches, spun.

A parrot perched with tales so grand,
Said, 'This trunk's been to every land!'
With tales of pirates and a sea,
It spun adventures, wild and free.

The bark with patterns, oddly drawn,
Spoke of a night that went till dawn.
A raccoon nodding, so well-versed,
Declared a dinner feast rehearsed.

What a spectacle to behold,
A trunk that danced while legends told.
In laughter, life weaves an embrace,
Twisted tales in every trace.

## Echoes from the Forest's Heart

Deep within where shadows play,
A melody calls to join the fray.
Critters gather, a quirky song,
As moonlit glee all night prolongs.

Wandering whispers, slight and bold,
Speak of stories long retold.
Fungi don their party hats,
While beetles march like tiny sprats.

A chorus of chirps and gentle croaks,
In a symphony of friendly jokes.
Each note a quirk, each pause a twist,
In forest concerts, none can miss.

With fireflies glowing, guiding light,
The echoes dance through starry night.
As laughter ripples, true delight,
In the heart of woods, pure and bright.

## A Meeting of the Unusual Hues

Colorful whispers brush the ground,
In shades so odd, joy abounds.
The grass wears socks, a vibrant show,
While daisies gossip, 'Who's that glow?'

At twilight's gate, the hues collide,
A rainbow party that can't hide.
With splashes of laughter, mischief in air,
The flowers boast, none can compare!

A bluebird spins in swirling glee,
While a purple bush sings, 'Join with me!'
The wonders of colors, whimsical schemes,
Invite all critters to dance in dreams.

As day turns night, a sunset cue,
The sky dons stripes in every hue.
Together they find their merry crew,
In a world where oddness feels like new.

## **Nature's Offbeat Ballet**

In the forest, squirrels prance,
Dancing wildly, take a chance.
Wobbly branches catch the sight,
As twirling leaves join the delight.

A rabbit hops on one-foot high,
While crickets croon and passersby.
The sun's a spot in shades of grin,
Who knew trees could truly spin?

Mushrooms wear their polka dots,
While toads throw parties by the pots.
A frog in tutus leaps with glee,
Twirling through the canopy.

Nature's laughter fills the air,
With each twist, a surprising flair.
In the wild, no step's a bore,
Join this dance; who could want more?

## The Whisper of Anomalous Breezes

A gust wiggles through the trees,
Tickling leaves with playful tease.
They gossip tales from far and wide,
As petals flutter, all abide.

In the windy waltz of jest,
The acorns roll, they pass the test.
A breeze that sneezes with a giggle,
Makes the flowers sway and wiggle.

Dandelions dream of flight,
While fairies dance in sheer delight.
With whispers high, they tease the rain,
In this odd breeze, there's no refrain.

Branches shake in laughter's grasp,
As nature whispers, we just gasp.
Anomalies in every sound,
In these breezes, joy is found.

## Paradox of the Growing Stump

A stump declared it wished to grow,
Told the trees to take it slow.
'I'm unique with this brown hat,'
Said the stump, while snaring a rat.

Around it gathered all the bugs,
One crickets' shout, 'Hey! Let's hug!'
They cheered this strange remaining log,
Which danced to sounds of the morning fog.

Except the ants, who thought it wrong,
To stack their homes on roots so strong.
The stump just chuckled, 'Is it all,
To be a tree? Let's have a ball!'

A paradox of roots and dreams,
Who knew stumps could have such schemes?
In laughter, nature speaks in jest,
As oddities put laughter to the test.

## Dreams from the Tangling Vines

In the tangle of the vine,
Bees in hats toast sips of wine.
A party planned for every critter,
With laughs and songs, none to jitter.

Lizards wear their vibrant thrills,
While mice serve snacks and tiny frills.
The vines create a swinging stage,
Where dance moves spark, defy the age.

As moonlight patches spark the scene,
The garden bursts into a dream.
With giggles floated through the night,
All creatures join in pure delight.

When morning breaks, the party fades,
Yet whispers of fun still cascade.
In tangled dreams, we find our fun,
For nature's jest has just begun.

## The Harmonies of an Eccentric Eden

In a grove where squirrels dance,
And tulips wear polka dots,
The giggles of the breeze prance,
While bees buzz in funny spots.

A cat with a top hat meows,
As shadows play silly tricks,
The frogs in waistcoats take vows,
To charm with their quirky licks.

An owl in spectacles reads,
While dancing to the tree's beat,
Sowing outrageous little seeds,
Of laughter beneath their feet.

Here mushrooms sing in bright hues,
And every branch tells a tale,
Where whimsy ignites in queues,
Of oddness that will never stale.

## The Uncharted World Within Green

Amidst the ferns, a parade waits,
With snails donning party hats,
They line up in curious states,
While owls juggle acorn fats.

A rabbit wears mismatched socks,
Chasing shadows of its feet,
While dancing on slippery rocks,
And the grass echoes a beat.

Leaves whisper secrets of fun,
As beetles play hopscotch in rows,
The sun sets in a cheeky run,
Making shadows put on shows.

In this realm of leafy delight,
Where giggles and chortles blend,
The world spins with sheer delight,
In a dance that will never end.

## **Anomalies Between the Leaves**

There's a lizard with a bowtie,
Sipping tea from a tiny cup,
While ants in tuxedos fly,
With cake on the side up.

Whimsical clouds float by slow,
Juggling dreams as they drift,
And the trees, in a cheeky row,
Share secrets that make minds lift.

Goldfish swim in puddles wide,
Trading stories with the winds,
While butterflies laugh and glide,
In a world that never rescinds.

Hiccups of giggles arise,
As nature sings out its song,
With winks and quirky surprise,
In this place where we belong.

## Echoes of Unconventional Winds

The wind carries whispers of cheer,
As dandelions play leapfrog,
Each gust brings a chuckle near,
And robins dance on a log.

A raccoon juggles shiny spoons,
While mushrooms wear silly hats,
The night hums absurd tunes,
As laughter breaks out in spats.

Branches sway with giddy glee,
Tickling the clouds up high,
In this riotous jubilee,
Where oddities never say goodbye.

Echoes of joy fill the air,
As the moon waves a bright grin,
In this world where no one can care,
For oddities just begin.

## Shadows of the Mighty

In the shade of giants, we gather with glee,
Where the mighty shadows dance, wild and free.
Squirrels hold court, in their tiny tuxedos,
While the wise old owl sings lullabies to me.

Under the branches, a picnic unfolds,
With sandwiches bravely challenged by ants bold.
A raccoon in glasses reads a map upside down,
Confidently exploring his make-believe town.

Frolicking foxes juggle acorns with flair,
While a hedgehog in glasses combs through his hair.
In the time of the trees, let's celebrate odd,
For every great shadow harbors a nod.

## Leaves of Legend

A leaf fell down, spinning tales in the breeze,
Of fairies and wizards, and giggling trees.
The wind whispers secrets of ants in a mess,
And a turtle who thought he could learn to impress.

At night the leaves glow, with glimmers of light,
As chipmunks breakdance and squirrels take flight.
In this leafy arena, laughter dominates,
With echoing giggles from slumbering mates.

Curious creatures discuss "who's really the best?"
As the moon makes its rounds in a sparkly vest.
The legends grow taller with each whispered tale,
In a forest where humor rides on the gale.

## The Woodland's Hidden Tales

In shadows of green, stories twist and twine,
Of a porcupine prince who thinks he can shine.
A joyful frog croaks, "I'm the king of this bog!"
While birds gather 'round, joining in with a fog.

A critter parade marches on with a cheer,
Wombats in capes bring the holidays near.
They sing of the silly, the strange, and the rare,
Of a weasel who dreams of becoming a bear.

Excitement abounds in this woodland bazaar,
With critters in costume, oh, how bizarre!
Legends worth telling, absurd and surreal,
In laughter and joy, the forest will heal.

## Boughs of the Unexpected

When branches twist sideways, they tickle the sky,
With raccoons in top hats, oh my, oh my!
A squirrel with a ukulele sits to perform,
His songs full of humor, they break every norm.

The acorns all chuckle, as creatures converge,
In a clamor of antics, their laughter will surge.
A hedgehog declares, "I'm the funniest beast!"
While the wise owl nods, "You are a true feast!"

Unfurled in the twirled, fairy tales live,
With punchlines galore, joy is what we give.
In woods filled with wonders, the unexpected thrives,
As laughter and magic bring smiles to our lives.

## Quirks of the Treefolk

In shades of green, the gossip flows,
The squirrels dance in silly clothes.
With acorn hats and tiny socks,
They prance about like funny clocks.

A raccoon juggles pine cone treats,
While owls watch with laughing beats.
A parrot squawks a joke or two,
And tree trunk fairies join the crew.

When sunlight gleams in gilded beams,
The bunnies plot their playful schemes.
They leap and tumble, what a sight,
In this enchanted, merry light.

Each branch a stage, each leaf a cheer,
The woodland folks hold laughter dear.
With every giggle, roots will sway,
Life here is just a game to play.

## Treasures in Twisted Branches

Among the boughs, a treasure's found,
A wobbly hat spins round and round.
A kite caught high in tangled leaves,
Makes for fun, as laughter weaves.

A rabbit's sock hangs from a twig,
A sight so silly, it makes us gig.
A squirrel's feast of old shoe lace,
A feast of joy, a chuckle's grace.

The shadows dance with giddy glee,
As squirrels share their recipe.
For acorn pie and berry stew,
Such strange delights, a funny brew.

Each twist and turn has secrets told,
In gnarled branches, hearts unfold.
They celebrate the odd and rare,
Adding wonder to the air.

## Echoes of the Forest Floor


On the forest floor, a giggle hides,
Among the leaves where mischief bides.
A froggy sings a daring tune,
As mushrooms dance beneath the moon.

A hedgehog with a feathered hat,
Invites the bugs to dance and chat.
They twirl around, they laugh and sway,
A merry band that loves to play.

A tumbleweed rolls in with flair,
Chasing a squirrel without a care.
They tumble down a leafy hill,
A joyous echo, time to thrill.

With every sound, a laugh is spun,
As critters gather, the fun's begun.
Amidst the oddities of the floor,
Life brings a smile forevermore.

## Wondrous Wonders on the Wind

The whispers of the wind do tease,
With secrets only trees appease.
A leaf that rides on breezes light,
Turns summer days to pure delight.

A dandelion, with poofy dreams,
Launches fluff like silly beams.
It tickles noses, makes them sneeze,
A giggling gale dances with ease.

The bees buzz jokes from flower to flower,
While butterflies in laughter tower.
A raccoon plays tag with the breeze,
As everyone tumbles beneath the trees.

With every gust, a chuckle rings,
Such wondrous wonders the wind brings.
In playful swirls, their joy will blend,
In nature's laughter, there's no end.

## Hidden Tales of the Old Knots

In the grove where whispers hide,
Knots of stories twist and glide.
Squirrel chats with ancient bark,
Beneath the shade, a lark's remark.

Dancing shadows round the tree,
With laughter loud, yet none can see.
A raccoon juggles acorns high,
While grumpy turtles pass on by.

Each branch wears a hat of moss,
Where every critter cues a toss.
Upside down, the world's a game,
And nature's odd, but who's to blame?

Through twisted roots and knotted tales,
The hidden humor gently trails.
A secret world in every nook,
Come take a peek, just take a look!

## Eloquent Silence of Nature's Oddities

Among the leaves, a quiet grin,
Where talking toads often begin.
A butterfly with a top hat on,
Flaps through meadows 'til the dawn.

Caterpillars knitting sweaters tight,
Debating if they'll take to flight.
The sunflowers nod, they're in the game,
With blooms that laugh, yet not the same.

A brook giggles past, a ticklish stream,
While shadows waltz in a whimsical dream.
Lizards wear spectacles, wise and old,
Spinning tales of legends bold.

The forest hums a funny tune,
A riddle wrapped in golden rune.
In silence, nature finds its fun,
A grand performance just begun!

**The Harmonious Chaos of Roots**

Roots like dancers twist and spin,
In a rhythm where dreams begin.
Wiggly worms do the tango there,
While slugs play trumpets, unaware.

Tangled webs of joy and glee,
Seeds plot mischief, can't you see?
A rabbit pulls a prank so sly,
While fireflies twinkle in the sky.

Nature's orchestra's out of tune,
With drumming frogs beneath the moon.
Branches swing in wobbly lines,
Making music of all kinds.

In every knot, a secret lives,
Where the chaos softly gives.
With roots embracing all that's strange,
The forest sings, and hearts exchange!

## Charm of the Uncommon Tree

In a corner where whimsy grows,
Stands a tree that surely knows.
With polka dots and stripes so bright,
It's the life of every forest night.

Raccoons twirl in leafy skirts,
While crickets chirp in quirky spurts.
A wise owl gives a cheeky wink,
As bubbling brook joins in the blink.

Branches stretch like lazy legs,
Holding up a nest of dregs.
Past the boughs, the laughter rings,
And even spiders wear funny strings.

The charm of oddity's alive,
Where painted leaves can surely thrive.
A spell of giggles in the breeze,
Join the dance beneath the trees!

## The Strange Fruit of Curiosity

In the meadow ripe with cheer,
Bouncing berries disappear.
A fruit that giggles, oh so sly,
It tickles noses, oh my, my!

In the shade, a riddle grows,
A loaf of bread with purple toes.
It whispers secrets, what a tease,
While squirrels dance just to please!

Jellybeans in the grass do prance,
Hopping high in sugar's dance.
A slice of pie with eyes so wide,
Oh, what joy on this wild ride!

The oddest feast you ever see,
With bounce and jiggle, full of glee.
Each curious bite, a merry tune,
The laughter echoes 'neath the moon!

## **Moonlit Revelations of the Grove**

Under silver beams at play,
Frogs in hats sing songs of sway.
They frolic 'round the ancient trees,
With whispered laughs and summer breeze.

Bats in capes tell tales so wild,
A merry band of nature's child.
Where shadows stretch and giggles roam,
The woods become a lively home.

In the nooks, a gnome sits tight,
His pet goldfish glows so bright.
Together they share snack and brew,
With fireflies dancing, just for two!

As night draws in, the wonders swell,
With winks and nods, they weave their spell.
They spin a world of playful jest,
Where midnight magic feels the best!

## The Antics of Woodland Spirits

In the glen, with mischief rife,
Sprites play tricks, they love this life.
They swap the acorns for confetti,
And laugh as squirrels go all jetty.

Dancing round the toadstool stage,
Fairies write the funniest page.
With twinkling eyes, they plot and scheme,
As tadpoles join in on the dream.

A rabbit dons a tiny crown,
Declaring he's the smartest around.
While raccoons serve their fanciest brew,
To toast the antics that ensue!

At dusk, they prance, a merry sight,
Spirits twirl in pure delight.
With laughter ringing, hearts entwined,
In this green haven, joy we find!

## Portraits of the Peculiar

A tree with glasses, so wise and grand,
Paints portraits of the whimsy band.
Each branch a brush, each leaf a stroke,
Capturing laughter in every joke.

The flowers grin with vibrant hues,
Dancing to the buzzing muse.
They prance in tandem, colors clash,
In the garden where oddities splash!

A frog with shoes, so neat and slick,
Dances with charm, oh what a trick!
With every leap, a new surprise,
As squirrels chuckle, and owls rise.

These masterpieces of nature's hand,
Stitching stories in the land.
So come and wander, don't delay,
In this quirky world where oddities play!

## Portraits of Peculiarity

In the park, a squirrel wears shades,
Reckless and bold, in the sun he parades.
A pigeon with style, sporting a hat,
Waddles with swagger, like a fancy cat.

Trees gossip softly in rustling leaves,
Sharing their tales of tricksters and thieves.
A toad in a tux, he croaks a fine tune,
While ants organize, plotting a heist 'neath the moon.

A butterfly juggles while bees buzz around,
Cheering for gnomes hidden deep in the ground.
Each branch holds secrets, it seems they conspire,
To tickle the whims of the playful and dire.

So come and explore, with laughter and glee,
The curious world nestled under the trees.
For in every shadow, a quirk can be found,
In the whispers of nature, odd joys abound.

## **Sylvan Mysteries Unraveled**

Beneath the tall trunks, a fox plays a tune,
With a mouse on the flute, under gaze of the moon.
A deer in a tutu dances with flair,
As rabbits take selfies, in bright springtime air.

Trees wear costumes of luminous green,
Transforming the forest into a grand scene.
The mushrooms join in with a colorful show,
Twirling and whirling, oh what a glow!

Squirrels paint portraits with acorns and twigs,
While owls roll their eyes at the antics of jigs.
Each nook a surprise in this woodland delight,
Where laughter erupts in the heart of the night.

So grab your own gnome, join the whimsical spree,
Where oddities flourish, nature's jubilee.
In the embrace of the trees, let laughter bestow,
The joy of peculiar, now watch it all grow!

## The Chronicles of Unseen Life

A wizardly crow flies with a wand made of twine,
Casting spells on the breeze, how utterly divine!
A porcupine juggles, his spines in a spin,
While frogs in tuxedos are ready to win.

Ladybugs gossip about the latest craze,
As flowers gossip too, their petals ablaze.
Down the lane, a hedgehog gives fashion advice,
His quills standing sharply, looking oh so nice.

With capes made of leaves and hats made of bark,
The critters convene for a grand evening lark.
A whimsical tournament of silliness arises,
With laughter and cheers, amidst night's surprises.

In this realm of the strange, where the tiny unite,
Each moment a treasure, the ordinary takes flight.
So let your heart open, and join in the fun,
For the tales of the unseen have only begun!

## Legends Woven in Green

In the heart of the grove, a turtle tells tales,
Of witches and wizards who ride on the gales.
He spins yarns of fairies, all glitter and cheer,
As the wise old raccoon lends a skeptical ear.

A grassy green dragon does yoga at dawn,
While crickets applaud with a soft, soothing yawn.
Lavender breezes will tickle your nose,
As hedgehogs debate 'bout the best scent of prose.

Through branches and brambles, the rumors take flight,
Of a squirrel who dreams to become a great knight.
Frogs sing the ballads of lost wooden shoes,
In this intriguing place, where the odd is your muse.

So gather your friends, bring a grin or a grin,
In this kingdom of green, the adventure begins.
Where laughter is woven, and fun is the thread,
In the legends of life, let joy be widespread!

## **Whispers of Ancient Trees**

In the garden where squirrels play,
Leaves gossip secrets, come what may.
Branches twist in a silly dance,
Bugs prance about, lost in a trance.

A wise old trunk tells tales at dusk,
Of daring dreams and playful husk.
With acorns dropping like little bombs,
Laughter echoes, the air just warms.

Twigs overhead make a creaky song,
As critters frolic, all day long.
Mice chat loudly about the breeze,
While shadows stretch beneath the trees.

All around, the world feels bright,
In this woodland of pure delight.
Nature's jesters, so wild and free,
Share their humor with you and me.

## Secrets Beneath the Canopy

Under the branches, mysteries hide,
Where chipmunks chatter, full of pride.
A slow snail races, or so he claims,
As wiggly worms play name-the-games.

Mushrooms giggle with colorful glee,
In their own circus, they love to be.
Fungi fashion little hats of charm,
Waving to hedgehogs like a friend-to-arm.

Beneath the leaves, a ruckus brews,
With whispers of magic, quirks, and hues.
Rabbits giggle at riddles of old,
In this merry realm, both brave and bold.

Vines wear laughter like a gown,
As sprites twirl amid the grass so brown.
Nature's comedy steals the scene,
In a grove where nothing's routine.

## The Uncommon Grove

In a grove where shadows twist and sway,
Trees don sunglasses, chill all day.
With wobbly roots that tickle the ground,
And laughter echoes, a merry sound.

A beetle boasts of his slick new ride,
While critters gather, full of pride.
Each bark bears a noble tale or jest,
It's a gathering where giggles never rest.

Daisies discuss the latest trends,
Communicating like lifelong friends.
A misplaced acorn starts a debate,
On who could win in a dance-off plate.

Here, squirrels wear capes, a sight to see,
In this land of whimsy, wild and free.
No leaf untouched by gleeful cheer,
As fun takes root, year after year.

## Curiosities in the Orchard

In an orchard where oddities bloom,
Apples whisper of impending zoom.
Peaches giggle when the sun's too bright,
As lemons plot a way to take flight.

A worm claims he's a master chef,
Cooking stories on each leafy clef.
While cherries bounce to the rhythm's thrum,
Creating a chorus of utmost fun.

In the shadows, the pears play tricks,
Rolling around with acrobatic flicks.
A squirrel dressed in polka dot ties,
Teaches the apples to improvise.

Under twisted branches, the laughter swells,
In this delightful patch where whimsy dwells.
With each bite of fruit, a story unfurls,
In this odd little world, where strange joy twirls.

## Groves of Enchantment

In a forest, a squirrel pranced,
With acorns on his head, he danced.
A fox in glasses read a book,
While rabbits shared a laughing look.

A mushroom wore a tiny hat,
A hedgehog sat and talked with a cat.
The trees whispered secrets, quite absurd,
As a parrot sang, without a word.

A gnome slipped on some freshly dew,
And fell into a bowl of stew.
Fireflies flashed like stars on cue,
A party formed, as nature grew.

But who would guess, in such a place,
That laughter hides behind a face?
With wonder sprouting from the ground,
In this grove, joy's always found.

## The Unexpected Bloom


A flower sprouted with bright pink shoes,
And danced around, hearing happy tunes.
With petals that twirled like a ballet,
It caught the sun's rays, brightening the day.

A bee in a top hat buzzed around,
In search of the sweetest nectar found.
It joined the flower in a showy jig,
With moves so wild, like a dancing pig.

A carrot dressed in bright green threads,
Took a leap, as the daisies said,
"Come join our fun, don't be so shy!"
With laughter echoing, up to the sky.

The hill was alive with funny sights,
In this garden of peculiar delights.
Nature's stage, a whimsical room,
Revealed the charm of the unexpected bloom.

## Dancing with the Unknown

A tree was seen doing the cha-cha,
While shadows giggled, who's that? Ha-ha!
Branches swung, no rhythm denied,
As leaves fell softly like confetti wide.

A lizard in a tutu tried to leap,
Over puddles where reflections sleep.
With every spin, he slipped with grace,
Giggling made him forget the race.

The clouds drifted in a funky beat,
As raindrops tapped like little feet.
The sunset glowed with colors bright,
Inviting all to dance in light.

Yet in one corner, quite aloof,
A grumpy rock declared, "What goof!"
But magic swirled around in mirth,
In every nook, love filled the earth.

## Whims of Nature's Canvas

On a canvas made of leafy greens,
Where shadows danced like funny scenes.
Acorns painted polka dots,
While squirrels played in silly spots.

A rainbow snail slid past with glee,
Its shell adorned with sprightly spree.
It left a trail of sparkly light,
As sunbeams giggled at the sight.

A beetle juggled tiny stones,
It balanced well, but heard some groans.
For birds above began to squawk,
"Hey, down there, don't block the walk!"

With all these quirks, a scene so bright,
Nature laughed with sheer delight.
In every corner, whimsy swayed,
In this unique art, all joy displayed.

## The Unique Tapestry of Life

In a garden where socks grow in pairs,
Laughter floats up from strange wooden chairs.
Kites dance and swirl with a chattering glee,
As mushrooms play chess with a bumblebee.

A rhubarb brigade leads the way on a stroll,
Wearing tiny top hats, they've taken control.
While cabbages gossip beneath leafy hats,
Discussing the quirks of the old, wise old cats.

A pickle parade marches right down the lane,
As frogs in bowties join in the refrain.
Giggling squirrels juggle acorns with flair,
While the sun paints the skies with a vibrant air.

So come join the fun in this whimsical place,
Where whimsy and wonder share a warm embrace.
For life is an oddity, a curious thrill,
Full of giggles and quirks, and always a chill.

## Surreal Shadows Among the Trees

Whispers of shadows dance under the moon,
Giant carrots play jazz while a fish hums a tune.
The owls wear glasses, reading books upside down,
While the raccoons plot to steal the town crown.

In the subtle twilight, the giggles ignite,
As gnomes in the bushes have a late-night fight.
They toss around acorns, arguing their score,
While the crickets keep time with a tap on the floor.

Dandelions sway, wearing shades oh so bright,
As bumbles in pajamas buzz off into night.
The trees chuckle softly, their roots all entwined,
In a world where the quirky thrives unconfined.

So skip through the forest where oddities grow,
Embrace every odd, let your laughter flow.
For in the surreal, the shadows will tease,
And weave all their tales with the curling of leaves.

# Chronicles of the Strangely Grown

Once sprouted a pickle who fancied himself wise,
He debated with carrots under vast, open skies.
With tails like spaghetti and beans in the fray,
A vegetable summit unfolded each day.

Across the leaf-strewn, cobblestone tracks,
Roamed beets with capes, plotting daring attacks.
While peas in a pod formed a rock band of sorts,
Xylophones made from tin cans, such crafty cohorts.

Though tomatoes were timid, they gathered their might,
And facilitated arguments way into the night.
As celery stalks tapped to a rhythm unheard,
Conspiring to conquer with thoughts that were blurred.

Comical tales of the strange ever bloomed,
In a garden where whimsy always resumed.
Together they laughed at their silliness found,
In a world full of strange shapes spinning around.

## The Curious Cadence of the Forest

In a grove where odd critters do chatter away,
You'll find turtles in tuxedos deciding to play.
Grasshoppers run races in shoes made of foam,
While the trees hum a tune that feels like home.

A flamingo bakes cookies, now isn't that sweet?
With a dash of confusion and a sprinkle of beat.
The raccoons ride bikes with their tails in a spin,
As a wise old owl watches, ready to grin.

Silly shadows prance in the dim forest light,
While hedgehogs wear bowties and delight in the night.
They spin tales of adventures, both silly and grand,
Of mischievous misfits who all make a stand.

So dance with the creatures, just follow the beat,
Join the quirky parade on your two little feet.
Where every odd moment a memory calls,
In the curious rhythm of the enchanted halls.

## A Crown of Peculiar Stories

In a garden where tall tales grow,
A snail wore a crown, stealing the show.
The flowers would laugh, dance with delight,
As the sun shared secrets, glowing and bright.

Beneath a berry bush, gossip did swirl,
A frog donned a cape, oh what a pearl!
He croaked out a tune, the crickets would cheer,
While the wise old owl winked and drew near.

A squirrel with shades, on a branch took a seat,
Juggled acorns for fun, what a quirky feat!
With every brave toss, the audience gasped,
As the wind joined the act, leaving us clasped.

In this world of odd, laughter held sway,
Where quirky creatures brightened the day.
Stories spun round, like leaves in the breeze,
Each tale a delight, a curious tease.

## Mysterious Beneath the Cracked Shell

A turtle once pondered beneath his dome,
If his home was a castle, where should he roam?
He peeked through a crack, and what did he find?
A pancake parade of the silliest kind!

The grumpy old snail, with a hat made of fluff,
Sighed at the antics, but secretly loved stuff.
The berries came marching, with giggles and grins,
While the raindrops joined in, like jubilant twins.

A crab with a trumpet played tunes by the shore,
As the waves danced along, they begged him for more.
With a flip and a clap, the tide made a splash,
And the beach, oh so vibrant, became quite the bash!

In this cracked little realm, where odd things align,
Each moment a treasure, each laugh a sign.
So when you embrace what seems strange or small,
You'll find joy in the quirks, and the laughter of all.

## Conversations with the Wind's Whimsy

The wind wore a hat, tipped low to the ground,
Whispering secrets in a giggly sound.
An acorn replied, with a voice oh so bold,
'Take me for a ride, let your stories unfold!'

A feathered brigade fluffed their plumes in delight,
As tales wrapped around them, twinkling at night.
From castles of clouds to rivers of cream,
They danced in the air, living the dream.

Beneath a broad branch, the wind found a tune,
The leaves swayed and rustled, a whimsical croon.
A raccoon in socks, took a seat by a tree,
Joined in with chuckles, as happy as can be.

In this whimsical chat, where oddity thrives,
Each laugh painted colors on the canvas of skies.
So when you hear breezes, remember their cheer,
For the wind holds the magic, and laughter is near.

## The Oddity of Stillness

In quiet corners where shadows entwine,
A hedgehog read stories of the divine.
With spectacles perched on his tiny brown nose,
He turned every page, a delightful prose.

The mushrooms kept giggling, sprouting in place,
While a banana peel slid with elegant grace.
They paused for a moment, stillness to share,
In this peaceful odd world, filled with rare flair.

A toadstool was king, in a court of bright sprouts,
As the fireflies flickered, casting small doubts.
They pondered the quiet, the humor it lent,
Even silence could burst, like a balloon's content.

So in the midst of calm, and all that's serene,
Embrace every oddity, both funny and keen.
For in stillness, there hides a giggle or two,
Waiting to spring forth, in the oddest of cues.

## The Narrative of Unruly Branches

In a forest where branches dance and sway,
A squirrel in a hat proclaims the day.
He juggles acorns, quite the sight,
While birds cackle with sheer delight.

The trees gossip with rustling leaves,
Spreading tales of the mischief he weaves.
A raccoon in boots shows up for the fun,
Beneath the bright rays of the flamboyant sun.

The branches twist in chaotic flair,
Creating shadows that hardly care.
A dog rolls by, wearing a grin,
While the clouds above begin to spin.

Each twist and turn, a story unfurls,
With laughter that echoes and twirls.
In this woodland of oddball cheer,
Every creature sings a song, oh dear!

## **Enchanted Roots of Whimsy**

Deep in the ground, roots start to laugh,
Tickling the soil like a playful gaffe.
They wiggle and giggle as the rain comes down,
A dance of puddles makes every clown frown.

A frog in a vest croaks out a rhyme,
Claiming he's a witness to stolen time.
While worms weave stories in their muddy bed,
A snail dons glasses, looking wise instead.

Mushrooms sprout up with silly hats on,
Debating with toads till the day is gone.
The roots of the trees hum a merry tune,
Echoing laughter under the bright moon.

Beneath the surface, hijinks abound,
With giggles and quirks all around.
As nature's oddities throw a mad bash,
The world above dances, a vibrant flash!

## **The Divergent Path of Grace**

A path meanders, twists, and bends,
Where flowers chat and good humor sends.
A hedgehog wearing shades strolls by,
Winking at butterflies fluttering high.

The gravel giggles beneath their feet,
Rolling stones, a rhythm so sweet.
Laughter erupts from a nearby stream,
Reflecting a sunbeam's whimsical beam.

A squirrel plays hopscotch with a crow,
While daisies watch the chaos unfold slow.
A signpost points in every direction,
Confusing lost travelers with sweet affection.

In this land of quirky design,
Happiness blooms like an excellent wine.
Each fork in the road a choice so grand,
Leading to fun in this merry land!

## Secrets of the Eldritch Canopy

High above where the branches weave,
Secrets are spun on a playful eve.
An owl in a bowtie tells tales so tall,
Of the night that danced at the ancient ball.

Twinkling stars peek through leafy shades,
Joining in laughter as the night parades.
A fox breaks in, wearing a funky cloak,
Sharing a riddle with a gentle poke.

Mysteries wrapped in vines and sprigs,
Whisking away worries like magic twigs.
Each rustle a whisper, each rustle a cheer,
Encouraging quirks to shed every fear.

The canopy echoes with giggles and sighs,
As branches share jokes in clever disguise.
Secrets spill out in a joyous parade,
Under the moonlight, laughter won't fade!

## The Curious Heart of the Grove

In a grove where whispers twirl,
Trees wear hats made of pearl.
Squirrels gossip, tails in a twist,
Laughing at things that don't exist.

A rabbit with spectacles reads a book,
While frogs in tuxedos play by the brook.
The moon sometimes winks, oh what a sight,
As shadows play tag with delight.

A raccoon in a bowtie sings a tune,
Trying to charm a forgetful raccoon.
The breeze joins in, a merry accomplice,
In the dance of this magical circus.

In this grove, logic takes a nap,
While acorns toss on a soft tree lap.
Every branch holds a secret or two,
Life's a jest in this quirky view.

## **Mythic Leaves and Strange Seeds**

Under leaves that sparkle and gleam,
Gnome feet shuffle, sparking a dream.
Pine cones giggle, rolling away,
As bugs tie knots in the sunlight's ray.

A sunflower wears a silly grin,
While a mossy rock claims it's a king.
Each root whispers tales of delight,
As the woods buzz with playful fright.

Top hats on mice, a tea party affair,
Nutty squirrels leap through the air.
With jam on toast, they nibble and snack,
In this land where oddities unpack.

Strange seeds sprout in mismatched hues,
Boys in blue and girls in shoes.
Life is a party, come join the spree,
In these woods where nothing's quite as it seems.

## **Whispers of the Ancient Grove**

A wise old tree hums a tune,
While critters gather by the moon.
A fox with spectacles makes a toast,
To the laughter that the night loves most.

Hedgehogs wear boots, don't ask why,
They dance in circles, oh me, oh my!
Kangaroos in hats bounce with flair,
In a world so funny, beyond compare.

A leaf fell down, dressed in bling,
Critters laughed, it was quite the thing.
The wind shared secrets, playful and bold,
In this grove where wonders unfold.

With every rustle, a chuckle ensues,
Beneath the stars, with its joyous muse.
Here in the night, humor hides away,
In whispers soft, it's a laughter buffet.

## The Eccentric Dance of Shadows

Shadows waltz under the crescent glow,
As leaf sprites twirl in a whimsical show.
A cat juggles acorns, leaping high,
While butterflies wear socks, oh my!

Whimsy rules in this enchanted nook,
With mushrooms that giggle by the brook.
Spiders spin tales in webs of lace,
As owls wear glasses just to keep pace.

Bouncing hedgehogs skip and cheer,
While trees laugh loudly, "Join us dear!"
Raccoons play chess with a sly little grin,
As the dance of this madness begins.

In the flicker of light where the joy does meet,
Every critter shuffles on tiny feet.
In shadows that sway, bright laughter swells,
A party of oddities that giggles and dwells.

## Beneath the Gnarled Canopy

Beneath the twisted branches wide,
Squirrels hold a council, side by side.
They plot to steal the acorn stash,
While birds below enjoy a splash.

The raccoons wear their masks with flair,
Throwing wild parties without a care.
Beneath the leaves, they dance at night,
With moonbeams casting fleeting light.

A wise old owl shares his best joke,
About a tree that thought it spoke.
Laughter rings through knots and leaves,
As nature rolls its playful sleeves.

In such a place of silly sights,
The critters find their wild delights.
So if you seek a funny view,
Look up, for they're all laughing too!

## Secrets Carved in Bark

Within the bark, old stories dwell,
A heart, a name, and some odd smell.
One tree claims to keep a secret,
Of how it tricked a passing beet.

Sprinkles of laughter float in the air,
As squirrels peek from laurel hair.
Each carving holds a gossipy tale,
Of how the branches sometimes fail.

Chipmunks debate the best design,
While ants parade in a straight line.
They map the best routes to the best snacks,
Hiding treasures on the mossy tracks.

With each new whisper, the stories grow,
Like branches twisting to and fro.
Mysteries buzz with comic flare,
In the funky trees that do declare!

## The Quirky Roots of Time

Roots like fingers reach and twist,
Grasping secrets none can resist.
They whisper tales of days gone by,
Of bees that danced and trees that sigh.

Each twisty root has its own song,
Of nature's weirdness all along.
They stretch and curl in funny ways,
Reminding us to laugh and play.

In this underground, they plot and scheme,
Chasing shadows like a silly dream.
A patchwork quilt of dirt and fun,
Where giggles echo, one by one.

As the seasons change, the roots confide,
In laughter, secrets cannot hide.
Digging deeper, they weave the rhyme,
Of stories lingered through the time!

## A Symphony of Knotted Branches

Branches twist like tangled hair,
Creating tunes that fill the air.
Joyful melodies of chirps and squeaks,
Where every turn brings silly peaks.

A songbird sings of missed high notes,
While rivers of laughter fill the throats.
Each note a tale of clumsy flights,
Under the canopy of merry lights.

Woodpeckers drum a catchy beat,
As rabbits hop and squirrels compete.
In this orchestra of leafy whim,
The instruments never fall dim.

So gather 'round, let's join the fun,
As leaves dance under the shining sun.
In knots of wood, life takes a chance,
Creating music with every prance!

## Timeless Chronicles of the Unseen

In the shade of a curious tree,
A squirrel wears glasses, sipping tea.
The branches twist, dance, and sway,
While acorns plot a nutty play.

Beneath a toadstool, a mouse finds gold,
A storybook wrapped in leaves, unfold.
The winds whisper secrets, bright and clear,
As turtles chuckle far and near.

A hedgehog in a hat counts the stars,
While fireflies gossip about Mars.
Each critter has tales full of cheer,
And laughter echoes, nowhere to fear.

With every step on the green glade,
Jokes and jests in the sun parade.
In this world where oddities cheer,
Funny surprises draw us near.

## Echoes of Whispers Past

An owl in a bowtie, sharp as a tack,
Sips cocoa while wearing a cozy hat.
Trees talk gossip of squirrels below,
In the hush where wild secrets flow.

The moon chuckles down with a glow,
As rabbits in tuxedos put on a show.
With each little hop and a daring twirl,
They dance 'neath the stars in a merry swirl.

The brook babbles tales of cats in capes,
While frogs debate about fanciful shapes.
In a world where odd meets the absurd,
Nothing is strange, and the joy's unheard.

In shadows, the whispers tickle the breeze,
As laughter abounds in tall, swaying trees.
Among the unseen, we safely roam,
Finding quirky treasures, we call home.

## Wandering Through the Eccentric Boughs

Under the branches so wide and spry,
A giraffe sneezes, oh my, oh my!
A parrot recites the news of the day,
As beetles in top hats begin to sway.

Acorns wearing shoes dance on their own,
And mushrooms play music, a curious tone.
Through honeycomb paths, giggles resound,
In this whimsical forest, joy is unbound.

A fox in pajamas juggles some stones,
While raccoons make mischief among wooden thrones.
With every odd twist of the enchanting route,
You'll find that each moment has something to shout.

Beneath the peculiar, laughter ignites,
As critters and trees share silly delights.
So wander with glee where the oddball things grow,
In a land where the fun simply won't slow.

## Quirks of the Forest Floor

At dawn, the mushrooms throw a ball,
Inviting all critters, both big and small.
The hedgehogs serve tea on plates made of leaves,
While the wind plays a tune, and everyone grieves.

Beetles in sneakers race down the lane,
Cheering for victory, loud in their gain.
While lizards all laugh in the sun's cozy light,
Spinning strange tales of a wild, wacky night.

In corners, the shadows giggle and tease,
While a snoring bear snoozes, filled with ease.
A garden of nonsense grows wild and free,
As oddities bloom like a fun-filled spree.

So tiptoe and twirl among roots and rocks,
For each step may surprise with peculiar knocks.
In this charming spectacle, boos and cheers soar,
Embrace every quirk on the forest floor.

www.ingramcontent.com/pod-product-compliance
Lightning Source LLC
Chambersburg PA
CBHW051659160426
43209CB00004B/961